Jeffrey Thomson's *The Country of Lost Sons* imagines a land where the aggrieved and the grieving come wounded together, across borders of time and nation, epochs of loss and resurrection. There, they are redeemed, if not in fact then in his poems' muscular music and flint-edged wisdom. So many things "hiss" in these poems—shoes, doors, paper, even grass—we sense the horror lurking within daily graces. It's this horror Thomson interrogates and then reinvents in the deadly flight of Philoctetes's arrow and his own son's small-fisted punch. Beneath the city's shattered walls—ours, after all—Thomson raises the "terrible blessing of hope."

—Kevin Stein

The Country of Lost Sons, Jeffrey Thomson's brilliant new book, shows the poet to be a man deeply read in western and world literature, a poet who sees the past and present, life and art, as inseparable, and yet this knowledge is never forced, never pretentious—just a vital part of life as we live it day to day. How else can we understand the joys and horrors we live except in the context of everyone's joys and horrors, the book seems to ask. That knowledge and the passion of its saying tips everything toward joy.

—Andrew Hudgins

The Country of Lost Sons

Poems

*For Pam —
With great love
and admiration. Thanks
for bringing me to
Columbia. What a
pleasure to see you*

9/16/04

Also by Jeffrey Thomson

The Halo Brace
Renovation

The Country of Lost Sons

Poems

Jeffrey Thomson

Parlor Press
West Lafayette, Indiana
www.parlorpress.com

Quotations from *Goodnight Moon* by Margaret Wise Brown, Illustrations by Clement Hurd, used by permission of HarperCollins Publishers. Text © 1947 by Harper & Row, Publishers Incorporated. Text copyright renewed 1975 by Roberta Brown Rauch.

"Puff the Magic Dragon." Words and Music by Lenny Lipton and Peter Yarrow. © 1963; Renewed 1991 Honalee Melodies (ASCAP) and Silver Dawn Music (ASCAP). Worldwide rights for Honalee Melodies administered by Cherry Lane Music Publishing Company, Inc. Worldwide rights for Silver Dawn Music administered by WB Music Corp. International Copyright Secured. All Rights Reserved.

Parlor Press LLC, West Lafayette, Indiana 47906

© 2004 by Parlor Press
All rights reserved.
Printed in the United States of America
SAN: 254-8879
Library of Congress Control Number: 2004101306

Jeffrey Thomson. 1967–
The country of lost sons : poems / Jeffrey Thomson
   p.   cm.
  1. Poetry. I. Title.

ISBN   1-932559-14-0 (Paper)
ISBN   1-932559-15-9 (Cloth)
ISBN   1-932559-16-7 (Adobe eBook)
ISBN   1-932559-17-5 (TK3)

Printed on acid-free paper.

Cover illustration: Pieter Breughel the Elder's *The Massacre of the Innocents,* courtesy of Kunsthistorisches Museum, Vienna

Parlor Press, LLC is an independent publisher of scholarly and trade titles in print and multimedia formats. This book is also available in cloth, as well as in Adobe eBook and Night Kitchen (TK3) formats, from Parlor Press on the WWW at http://www.parlorpress.com. For submission information or to find out about Parlor Press publications, write to Parlor Press, 816 Robinson St., West Lafayette, Indiana, 47906, or e-mail editor@parlorpress.com.

for Julian

. . . he will weep much, too late, when his people are perished from him.

—Homer, *Iliad*, XI, 764

Contents

Acknowledgments *xi*

Narrative 3
Design 5
Camera Obscura 7
Bu Topraklar Bizimdi: A Message from Lefkosa 9
The Coffeehouse War 11
My Wife's New Shoes 14
New Poem 16
Paris 17
Plato's Expulsion 18
The Plane Descending 20
To the Sparrows in LAX 22
The Wager 23
Job in Agony 25
Hector in Hell 26
The Buddha 27
Temptation 28
The Country of Lost Sons 29
Against Prognostication 31
Alcibiades Leaving North Avenue Beach 33
Domestic Gothic 34
The Lyric Eye 35
Untitled 37
Tables 39
Julian and His Father 41
November Conservation 43

What Odysseus Thinks   44
Terrible Gestures   45
Prayer   46
Goodnight Nobody   47
Evolution   55
Warning   56
He Arranges His Poems   57
Trust   59
Desire   60
Not Resurrection   61
York Harbor   63
An Elegy for the Living in Early Spring   64

Notes   67
Index of First Lines   69
About the Author   71

Acknowledgments

Grateful acknowledgment is made to the editors of the following magazines in which these poems first appeared, or are forthcoming, some in slightly different form:

Crab Creek Review, "Paris"
Flint Hills Review, "Tables"
Ginko Tree Review, "Desire" (as "My Own Desire")
Natural Bridge, The Lastica, Kosovo section of "Goodnight Nobody" (as "Lastica, Kosovo") and "The Country of Lost Sons"
New Delta Review, "Goodnight Nobody" (sequence)
Pittsburgh Post-Gazette, "Terrible Gestures"
Puerto del Sol, "Elegy for the Living in Early Spring" and "Plato's Expulsion"
Southeast Review, "Narrative" and "*Bu Topraklar Bizimdi*: A Message from Lefkosa"
Willow Springs, "The Coffeehouse War" (as "Postscript")

"Temptation" won the Master's Poetry Contest, 2002.

I am indebted to a number of people without whose help and support this book would never have occurred. Gratitude is due to Sherod Santos, Lynne McMahon, Tony Deaton, Penelope Pelizzon, Andrew Hudgins, Terri Witek, Anna Catone, Alan Shapiro, Robert Hass, Mary Jo Salter, and Terrance Hayes for their time, their friendship, and their invaluable assistance and expert critique. But, as always, the most well-deserved thanks is reserved for Jennifer Anne.

—*Jeffrey Thomson*

The Country of Lost Sons

Narrative

—for Andrew Hudgins

Because it all begins with story,
the telling around the fire tearing
itself free from wood's fingerprint,

the book open on the table beside
a pitcher quivered with Calla lilies
or a fragrant spray of Carolina jasmine

whose honey is said to poison bees,
perhaps I should begin with the U-boat cook
opening his ration box of socks

late in the war. These socks, charcoal,
delicate as shadows in his hands,
made from human hair. He slips

them over his rotten feet and flits
through the ringing narrows, the tunnel
of air he travels with and through.

Or because all narrative is about
the self, personal and florid,
maybe I should begin with the hole

I tore through the ice, star-shaped
and black, the plunge and gasp,
my galvanized saucer swaying beneath me

as the water gave way. I walked home
beneath wind-stripped sycamores,
my clothes frozen into a carapace,

a husk of ice and wind, beneath
which I could shift and move, somehow
preserved from the murderous world.

Design

In vain have I smitten your children.

—Jeremiah 2: 30

Bells of the Epiphany blend with sirens
and the timbre of traffic flowing through
the valley. The light stripes late winter

with the Lord's design when the sun
rises from behind the chock-a-block clouds,
bare trees staccato on hillsides substantial

with snow. It is written that the fulfillment
of the prophet is in the slaughter of the innocents,
streets swimming with black damask,

inconsolable women. In Breughel,
a quiet tuft of soldiers clumps
in the snow-filled street, their horses,

heads down, distanced like shy dogs.
Houses the ochre and orange of Lebanon
beneath a metal-colored sky and oaks

pruned to pincushions in the foreground.
(Gone is the rampage of Ghirlandaio,
women raking the glaze-faced soldiers,

blades raised and tiny bloody torsos
amid the frescoed blues and gingers
of the Roman peace.) The people

fan out into their homes, casual
and neat, and even the blood
on the new snow feels domestic.

But just off-center, one woman kneels
holding the corpse of her child,
an overlooked pietà in a subtle tableau

of slaughter. In the shadow
of the cathedral the lights
of the cruisers spot the snow,

and at the center of the wreckage
an empty space shaped suspiciously
like grief as a wet wind unravels

from the south bringing rain, fat drops
filling the snow with small holes
as traffic backs up to the river.

Camera Obscura

Sing sorrow, sorrow: but good win out in the end.

—Aeschylus

Japanese maples light up
the understory and asters'
royal arms rise above
the star-dark mulch
turning spring to fall,
earth to sky. After weeks
of late spring chill, suddenly
the wide wound of the sky.
What hope would find among
these generous leaves
is missing now, in these days
of pyre and ditch. A sense
of peace, a gathering
of larks beyond the window.

We are left with the grotesque
of negatives—a bus blown apart,
torn metal scorched white
as petals, a galaxy of climbing roses
throttling the fence outside Celebici,
women weeping around blast furnaces
in Trepca, their faces bone black.

In the *Agamemnon*,
it is the solitary herald
who asks the assembled elders,

*Why must a live man count
the numbers of the slain,
why grieve at fortune's wrath
that fades to break once more?*

He speaks in the echoing
hall of the camera obscura,
where honor turns to burning trees
and a young soldier bends
against his will to pitch a boy
over the remaining walls
of Troy, where oxen stand
on the watchman's tongue
and Agamemnon turns
to watch his arm, his own
as yet unbloodied arm
drive the knife into his daughter
whose buckled lips bit the wind
that rose above the ships like rage.

Bu Topraklar Bizimdi: A Message from Lefkosa

On the postcard, crescent and star
carpet the lunar hillside, spun
into a texture of scrub oak
and brushwood pine, whitewashed
to a delicate rose. The soldier,
olive drab as anywhere, balances
a Kalashnikov on his hip,
defiant as a woman in a doorway.
The caption turned physical
in the rotting green line
of Turkish Cyprus: trash and
sheet tin, ingots of concrete woven
into oil barrels shoveled full of dirt.

This is Persephone's world,
loss in the lace of rotting plaster
lining hollow bakeries, dawn
falling unrequited into window bays,
shallow doorways of piss and ruin.
In the distance, perhaps, a woman
at a piano playing the first chords
of Shostakovich's *L'Oiseau de Feu*
and, again and again, the sound
of Demeter's elegant weeping.

But what if we've got it wrong—
we're certain of Demeter's role,
the raging grief of the mother,

her anger spraying out in waves
of wilt and wither—but what if
Persephone ate that fruit
on purpose, the pomegranate
glowing in her hand like a cloud-veiled
twilight moon, ate because she loved
the milk-thick theater of shadows
that was her palace, the open-mouthed
vengeance of her throne?

The Coffeehouse War

In the coffeehouse
where I sit in the width
of my day off,

the girl behind the bar
sweeps the counter
into damp circles,

her buckskin hair
curling around her face
like parentheses,

an expression
of continuous afterthought.
The slow pull

of summer runs
deep beside me.
The door opens

in a wave of wet hot air.
There is the weight
of what needs

to be read hanging
above my head,
the giddy heft of Homer,

the triplets of Aeschylus
and a book by a friend
with its laughing dog cover.

I have hacked
my way into the *Iliad,*
into the rage and sad pain,

into the wet peal
of bronze on bronze,
the squeals of men

who lost their bowels
to the dirt, and hear the echo
of Nestor's censure

of Achilles on the silent TV
that glimmers in the corner.
In Priština, a mob celebrates

the war's end with fireworks—
saffron and gold,
a particularly Cyrillic red—

an architecture of fire
and smoke beyond
the silhouettes of buildings

pulled down
when the antiaircraft
lashed its dark lettering

across the sky.
Embers filter down
across the town—

this not quite Troy.
And somewhere,
some new Andromache

weeps for her child,
the last to go
over the walls (a postscript

in the closed earth)
beyond which wait
the terrible ships.

My Wife's New Shoes

My wife's new shoes hiss like cats
turning themselves into questions,
whispers. Her feet breathe
with every step as she moves
past the Douglas fir in our backyard—
its small, toothed cones dropping,
pattering on the heaped needles.

The world is like this sometimes,
I think, because her mind
is somewhere else—leaving
the dry cleaners, carrying
ghostly dresses in their slick sacks,
or holding onions in her fragrant hand,
or on the examination table listening
to the buzz of that second heart
in her belly.

The world is like this: the sound
of the wind in the fir's leaves of wire,
the air white with a wet, late snow,
the cold holding on in the corners
of the day even as daffodils pull
through the soil and ripple
green lawns with their golden chrome.

My wife worries and holds her belly.
The moony skin above her hips
tents and stretches from inside—
the sketch of some articulate desire

like ribs through the skin
of the antique, crucified Christ,
the cross from a Mexican church
we found in a shop in Hot Springs.
Only a torso—
                    the stumps of arms,
                    legs cut at the thighs,
convex chest and gaunt stomach,
ribs heaving out of the dry wood,
aching in the air above old Coke bottles.

My wife worries and holds her belly.
Small world, a room of liquid breath,
the sonnet of hips, tent of dreams.
She worries and holds her belly.
My wife holds her belly and worries.
The world is like this:
                        the ribs and
the stretch of the skin, like starvation,
the world is like this: the ribs and
the wood gray as a cat, the branches
of the alders bent under the weight
of this late snow and the ducks
that stretch their necks above
the black water that swallows
the snow, that is the absence of snow.
The alders are gray and gaunt along
the felt-green lawn where bundles
of cherry blossoms hang a pink mist
against the dark water, where the snow
turns and turns and disappears.

New Poem

This the point where it begins—
a new story so familiar I hesitate
to start it, sure you'll smile
with that touch of condescension
that says, we've all been *here* before:
the boy tearing his bloody way
into the loudbright world,
the father (honestly) sleepy,
the mother soaked with joy.

And how I want the narrative,
the story's arc roping out
like clothesline in a bright wind,
how I want it to function,
like a bridge, the distant shore
leafed out in rutty green, everything
rising out of the rotten dark.

But you know and I know
that's how they all start out—
the everyday light falling over
the transom, chirp and warble
outside the window, a world reborn.
That's how they all start out—
Begin again—elegies I mean.

Paris

I run through this feud all day
as the sun slides behind tree after tree,
the baroque shadows of day tracing
the curves of my son's sleeping face:
Hector, Patroclus; Achilles, Hector;
Paris, Achilles; Paris—Who kills Paris?
That fancy pants dandy. More human
than heroes in his tongue-rich desire.
Does he skate off, no longer necklaced
to his terrifying beauty? Does love's fury
hound him, turned out from the civilized,
some new scar raking his elegant chin?

It's Philoctetes, I learn, the wounded one,
Philoctetes the archer ducking behind
the shields of his aristocratic infantrymen
who planted an arrow to the feathers
in his alabaster side. Paris, amazed
at the iridescent ache of his own blood,
brought somehow out of burning Troy
to expire by the side of Oenone,
the nymph whose bitter love-
lorn heart refused to heal him. My story,
the way I want it, is his to live in:
moving between storm-tossed stones
on a distant shore. I want him
alive for reasons I cannot name. Perhaps,
because I know what becomes of beauty
these days.

Plato's Expulsion

—written on an unpaid Chicago parking ticket.

Every poet knows
the story: how Plato
in his tenth book

turned the poets out
of his Republic.
Plato's art

worked like the backs
of men striped
with sweat,

laboring with marble,
or women turning
furrows in earth

with small hoes.
It was the gates
of Hades

not Achilles' shield,
the artless emblem
negated in precise

abstraction.
His gates close
on a night lost

in floating
leaves lit spinning
in the streetlight,

a cupped hand
bent in touching,
the trills of a woman

whistling Bach,
long, whiskey-
colored light

cut to stripes
on a gray cell
wall, fat piles

of shit
smoldering
in the corner.

Ten thousand burning
trees, a wing,
this unflinching expulsion.

The Plane Descending

The plane descending
                        through the sky's collapse,
through an indigo
                lightshow,
                          split-fingered
lightning
          painting the clouds
                            colonnade,
the way the wing lights
                beat
                      against the dark,
small, too small,
            cabin pressure
                        holding steady.
I (always that lyric *I*—
              inventing
                      and pretending—
a fly vivacious
            between
                the window and the screen)
I want you
        to see this as fear,
                      I want
to make you feel
            that snap at the ribs
                        as the plane
drops
        to catch on the next swell
                      of air,

                the glue
                            inside your mouth
                                                    as the lightning
                rivets the purple sky.
                                        But such gesture
                                                            is foolish—
                you are comfortable
                                        where you are,
                                                            reading this,
                the soft lights
                            and the good chair,
                                                        late Beethoven,
                perhaps,
                        on the stereo.
                                        Or the comfortable jostle
                of the train
                            as it clatters
                                        down the trestle
                toward the river
                                    and the tunnel,
                                                        a skyline
                full of light
                            rising up behind you.

To the Sparrows in LAX

I am reading this into precision:
the severe distortion of their flight,
articulate smackings among the ficus.
Cells of honeycombed light
filter down on laptops and novels,
plastic-capped lattes, leftovers
and the elegant refuse of food.
That pivotal moment when
they skipped through sliding doors
and lighted in the ornamental,
quick as ash in the stale air.
The glass-ribbed stasis
that illuminates the modern world.

The Wager

—Judges 11: 30-40

Ends with angels roiling the air
linked arm in arm beneath
the pandemonium of their robes.
Ends when Jephthah promises God
death to the first thing
through his door. Of course
it's his daughter, his only child,
who meets him at the gates
with timbrels and with dances.

The sky's gaudy with them,
a rich mail against the clouds,
but they're not here to hide
your eyes, nor mine. It's God
who doesn't want to watch.
He'd as soon spend his time
wringing rain from ropes
of cloud, watching lambs
muscle free from ewes,
the wet slap in the clover.

He knows there's a hell alone
for fathers who consume
their children in impotent wagers
and at its center is a garden
of hunger, waste and bone.

She floats in the doorway, clothed
in the light of the morning sun.
In the dry wind branches
clack and hiss as the gates
close on her like teeth.

Job in Agony

It's always ashes and the blazing sun.
His tarnished skin. The rubble
of his wind-sacked home.

But the children—his second
round—when Job has been
restored, his fortune doubled,
when he has knuckled down
to the whirlwind and made oblation
for his friends before the Lord,
it's the children that concern me.

They are ten altogether and
they move through the gauze
of the new orchard in loud,
green waves. Petals flicker
in the layered light. Shadows
burnt into the grass, stretched
across the reworked earth.

They pass him by as the wind carries
to him the scent of the garden,
so rich with its wealth of ashes,
so heavy with the meal of bones.

Hector in Hell

It is Hector who lingers near
the wall, the stone bright
under the ten-year sun. He waits
when his son has been taken
from him, when Andromache
has turned her back
on him to raise the boy
within the walls of Troy. He waits there
before Paris rousts him.
He waits there and must hold
the moment carefully:
his son's screams
at the horse-hair plume
and bronze-ridged eyes
turned to a bubble of laughter
as he is tossed in the air.
The helmet set aside
on the cracked path.
Andromache watching
with shining eyes. He crosses
the threshold and stands now
in the lens of the story,
the noon sun targeting him
with his shadow, but in
the black thickets of Hades,
he will gently lift his son again
and be lifted with him.

The Buddha

—for Jack Gilbert

*Surely this world is unprotected and helpless
and like a wheel it turns round and round,*

he said. The leaves, their wealth falling
from the bodhi, become his various lives

spinning beneath the sun. Once, he slices
the wet flesh of melons, feasts on fish

large as logs. Once, his ribs keel up inside him.
Once, a dog licks at his ulcerated sores.

Once, in gratitude, he lays himself down
before a starving tiger, her seven newborn cubs

mewling around him in piles. There is one
remaining, one coin he cannot bear to squander.

He slipped out of his last life
like a thief; he could not wake his son

before he fled. It would have stopped him,
he knows, the poverty in his boy's smallest smile.

Temptation

> *Weep not just yet: for you must later weep*
> *For wounds inflicted by another sword.*
> —Canto 30

She has unwrapped the gates of hell,
but he wants her eyes like firelight
across the room, slow days in bed,
striped light across the sheets,
a braid of legs beneath. He wants
to dress her in the moonlight and
the exquisite twinge of her departure,
the skin behind her knee. He wants
the pleasure of her baking bread
in a stone-floored kitchen, deer
nuzzling the azalea buds beyond
the window. Dark rivers crossed
by white bridges. The undisturbed
air above their son's sleeping head.

But, when Beatrice first appears
in the garden high in Purgatory,
rafted down on angels' wings
and clothed in weeping flame,
Dante cannot meet her eyes.
He drops his gaze upon the Lethe—
dark and mirrored as the unforgiven
desire of Paolo and Francesca.
His reflection shames him once again.
In te, Domine, speravi—the words
of the psalm hauled up into the trees
by the angelic chorus. *Do you not know,*
she asks him, *that man is happy here?*

The Country of Lost Sons

—for Sherod Santos

In the ninth month of my son's life
I begin to dream of him
crushed beneath the wheels
of a fat panel van. In the quick

breath of terror that follows,
I know (*somehow*, in the *donnée*
of dreams) that he is not dead.
Is miraculously uninjured,

and the dream slips into
a caravan of lost worlds
and carnival gestures as I race
(purposelessly now) towards

the beckoning emergency room.
What is startling, as I wake,
is the ease with which I am pushed
from the velvet edge of this dream—

the horror that is equaled only
in its perfect clarity by the absolute,
gutty elation of his continuing breath,
the warm pucker of his soft mouth

I find, slipping out of bed and down
the moon-speckled hall to check
again each night. Later that week,
an early evening tinged with indigo,

the perfume of a thousand rhododendrons
flashing against the dark, wide shine
of the Willamette, listening to an old friend
read from his new book, that I hear

the words beyond the words,
the ragged blue-black edge to all this
easy, forgiving grief: *my son
is my elegy, waiting to be written.*

Against Prognostication

I have not written about my son's future,
not yet. How he will read and reread

the *Audubon Field Guide* and memorize each bird,
how he will wander off under dappled light

and return home in a squad car. Not because
I can't imagine the way he will carefully

hold his hand above his heart
after he has unfurled the skin

from his meaty thumb, or how he will rip apart
a frog hind legs to jaw and how he will feel after.

I have not talked about the day he will wrap
his friend's car around a tree and *somehow*

walk away, leaving the scene limping
home to sleep in bloody sheets.

Not out of fear, though this genealogy hints at it.
This reticence is caution not reprimand—

what can he learn, anyway, from such a history?
That day will still come when he opens his palm

above a flame and smells himself burning.
Perhaps, by then his father will be brave enough

to let him have his own life, but I will not say,
be comforted, for comfort comes at a price.

And I will not talk about what comes next:
a girl, a kiss, a field of grass. His thin heart

tearing as she leaves. That part of the story
is all anyone wants, denouement

and then the singing, operatic camerawork
pulling back to reveal his loneliness in the grass,

blue herons stalking through a salt marsh at sunset,
ten glaucous gulls and a black back on the gables

of the paintworks riding out a storm.

Alcibiades Leaving North Avenue Beach

The el track's staccato shadows,
and a wash of cold air. My son
counts cars, numb multiples
he's not quite sure of—
One two four five seven—numbers
ruled up like beads on a wire of fire
from Plato's higher planes,
the supple thought of order
that rises up from beauty,
his Warhol hair, the glow
of summer weeping off his skin.

Immediately, I am Alcibiades
on the beach, the wreckage
of the Athenian fleet before me,
Byzantium gone.

What can Alcibiades say
about circumstance? What order
place upon the world? Exile
and the Hellespont waiting,
an assassin already out the door.
Can I go back to pull him
back from the edge, reassemble
him there on the platform
of the Ravenswood el?
It is love alone that lets me
let him enter the car, the vicious hiss
as the doors fold back,
their flat shine against the sky
as the train slips through the air.

Domestic Gothic

The sound of my son asleep
in his bed, the recurrent chirr
of his breath, is the sound
of my wife brushing her hair,
pulling the smoky length of it
across blades of weak light,
the sound of the last of the leaves
rotating in the cold glamour
of autumn, foxes chirruping
in their hillside den high
above our home, shovelfuls
of dirt returning to the earth
as dark and mucked with gold
as a swarm of bees clutched
in the churning orchestra
of their hive, strumming
desperately to stay warm.

The Lyric Eye

I, I start,
        charting the effect
                before
the buzz,
      like caffeine,
              carries
the poem
      down river,
              the froth and churn
of water
      over the spillway
              beside
a welter of osier,
        the orchestra rising
from its seat
      to bow
            before it begins
beneath
      gold leaf
            and brocade.
I, I begin,
      and already
            I am stifling
a yawn.
      I've heard this
            all before—
I bore myself,
      groveling
           for change,

        on the pavement,
                    this I,
                              surviving
on day-old
            tossed back
                        behind the bakery,
my clothes
            ironed with grime
                              and the smell
of piss,
            where I missed
                        one night
on a nasty binge.
                  All I want's
some charity,
            brother,
                      sister,
won't you help?
                  Toss a little attention
in this rattling
            cup.
                      Just look my way.

Untitled

Sunlight reflected
                off the puddle
                              on the slate
back steps,
        the remains
                of a late rain
on stone I laid
        by hand
                (the wet saw
that cut each to fit
            left its grit
in the basin
        like waste spun
                in a gold pan),
that light hits the ceiling
            and the last drops
from the hawthorn
          or the gutters
                  full
and overflowing
        cast ripples
                on the ceiling
as if the floor's invisible
            and in the bedroom
                    now
the rain keeps falling.
            There's no message here,
no one's dead,
        my wife and I
                aren't splitting up,

        the weather isn't reading us
                                better than
we read ourselves.
                        If she were here,
I might call to her
                        and lead her
                                        up the stairs
to lay down
                in the clean light,
                                        the trees ticking
around us
                like a collection of clocks,
                                        but
she's at work and I'm alone,
                                and how this turns
to story I can't say.
                        The slate means little
more than effort
                        and pride
                                and the light means
less than that.
                The rain has stopped
                        and you're on your own.
The careful drip
                of meaning
                                falls on the act
of making and unmaking
                                alike,
as flocks of starlings,
                        flecked with gold
wash around a tree-soaked sky.

Tables

My father sanding ash,
the hiss of paper
in his austere fingers.

Scroll-worked legs scaffold
the drop leaf as he fits
the cross slats flush against

the parson's trestle; this
quadrant, a span of space,
his table's frame framing

absence, waiting for the final
one-by-eights shaped to curve
slightly at the center.

The paper hisses with the grain.
He holds the wood so gently.
He breathes the dust.

With tongue and groove
he shapes the table's face . . .
All this, useless, useless.

This winter light.
This winter light is full of dust
and the room smells of oil,

varnish, stain. Did I wait
all afternoon, watching
the stacked boards become

a table—the ash glowing
like candlelight—or did I leave
my father there, his temples

catching dust and turning
gray, his breathing creased
by asthma? It is late

in the century. A flight
of jays tearing at cones
in the jackpines.

Light rain fills the branches
with its beautiful hands.
I have accomplished nothing.

Julian and His Father

—Little Sand Lake, Wisconsin

೧

The lake burnished
with late light,
he stands barefoot

on the ashen boards
of the dock, recognizing
even in midsummer

the chill of the water
he will enter and split
with the flat fins

of his hands.
As he swings his arms
and pushes off,

he balances there
in the bright air,
carelessly aloft

above his own shadow.

೧

Shoulders above the water
he floats in the dazzle
surrounded by the laughter

of looncall from the far
end of the lake where
they've shaped their nest

from winddrift and loss.
He drops beneath the surface,
dives into the tannin dark.

At my feet he wrinkles through
the diamond-backed water
up toward the light.

November Conservation

Fall's first gold has gone to rust,
an almost smoky rose, as leaves
of English oak soak the hillsides
and someone has turned the beds
and dug celosia, cut back rafts
of black-eyed Susan, planted
pansies in the median near
the Highland Park bridge.
With one lavish gesture planted
hundreds of small flowers—carmine
and violet, a delicate lemon
with black tears like the eyes
of dogs. The roadside blooms
and trembles in the cold wind.

Under this mackerel sky the river
shoves itself downstream, oceanic,
as the bridge—its brawny boot black
giving way to rust—acquiesces
to gravity. The pansies flutter
in pools above the river's black banks
and the ruts of parallel rails, racks
of shattered cars. Late in the year
the world surrenders again, as,
on a bench below a shoulder
of revealed hillside, a nursing
woman bends her head,
her child's skull a moon
against the used and tired air.

What Odysseus Thinks

When you have been a long time gone,
the streets shrink to meet you

on the drive home through leafy allées,
past squat bungalows of brick and stucco,

the flaring trumpets of Greek revival;
when the blunt angles of the setting sun

strike your face with something
that no longer feels like light and turns

the whole world bas-relief, it is easy
to believe in coming home free

of the weight of our various lives,
but hard, *too hard*, to see

the lights in some sudden windows
crying welcome, or fear.

Terrible Gestures

It has happened again.
As the planes slammed
into the silver towers
and the smoke wept out
like solder bannered
in the wind, as the steel
got weak in the knees,
a man and a woman—
strangers, lovers, perhaps
friends, does it matter?—
came together in the torn
burning, in the trembling
and clamor of glass.
They held hands, each
small comfort to the other,
and stepped into the air.
They held hands
as they fell, a gesture
that leaves me no peace.
It has happened again,
this terrible blessing of hope.

Prayer

—December 11, 2001

When a late rain has turned
the last of the leaves into
a refuse of dun running through
the corners of the evening,
when the generosity of light
is all but gone and the year's
eloquence has faded in a mist
of gritty dust, when nothing
remains but branches raked
against a cracked and splintered sky
and I would disappear into
the damaged dark, into the peace
of Cassandra, whose Greek
was mystic gibberish licked
with flame and the debris
of her ruined city, take from me,
Oh Lord, this bitter tongue
before I call out with her,
Make someone else, not me,
luxurious in disaster.

Goodnight Nobody

I

The late afternoon light settles down around them on the bed and my son stills—the first time all day. He is on his back on the bed, *Goodnight Moon* beside his head. My wife's voice articulate as sapphire in the air among the swoops of dust and light:

> *And a comb and a brush*
> *and a bowl full of mush*
> *And a quiet old lady*
> *who was whispering hush.*

Outside this room the world is all Kosovo. Mass graves and the arms of children in the rubble. In Lastica, the radio correspondent reports, Serbian militias were looking for one special girl. The town beauty. Unable to get their hands on her, "They took a 13 year old instead," remarks NPR.

It's the *instead* that gets me, really, the marking off of one life for another, that child taken and torn into beneath the wound-blue moon of her eye. The lucky one (with her "striking green eyes and black hair") squirreled away in borrowed, ratty clothes, hidden among a surprising weight of women. She survives to tell her story across the border in Macedonia. All the women gather together again.

The other one is hiding from us now, from all of us, an innuendo, an accusation fading back between the towers of sycamore, following the edges of the billowing hillsides. She waits in the wet grass that slaps at her broken feet, hoping to come home, but the *hiss* of that terrible word gives her up instead, its echo lingering in the voice on my radio.

II

Out walking the dogs, we pass a boy, seven or eight years old, who takes aim with a broomstick at a single engine Bellanca flying low. The sound of the plane taut in the sky. It dips its wings and turns into the wind to make the approach to the airport beyond the rim of elms that ring our park. The boy is enraptured. He aims with a broom and spits out the sound of automatic weapon fire between his swollen lips, following the plane's trajectory across the sky. The plane falls away toward the runway as if this small boy has actually shot it down.

III

My son is eleven months old and as I sit with him the television is on: CNN broadcasting from Kosovo. The image is antiaircraft above Priština. Shadowy crowds moving beneath the casement of the lens. Fires snapping in the streets.

Julian turns to the TV only when the commercials break in and, even then, only when there's music. When the Burger King cheeseburger soundtrack strikes up the *William Tell Overture* he turns to the set on his hands and knees and shakes like a dog with joy.

IV

When the sunlight piles into our bedroom in the late afternoon, full of dust, Julian reaches for it and wants, I think, to taste it. And when his hand come away empty, he'll try again. Sitting cinematically among his stacking blocks, he reaches for the black strap of the camera I am using to try to hold this moment. He pushes toward me. I put him back. He pushes toward me again and again I put him back, and suddenly my son turns away from me, his voice, rising and assembling itself in the air around him. It fills the small room, the lunatic sound of his anger. That anger that gives his life its life, a sudden white urgency among the chattering colors

Is this it? How we come to know that we know. The self suddenly beside the self, turned spectator in the theater of loss and anger.

V

He is trying to stand on his own. In the middle of the room on the soft rug, he'll stand up, wobble, and fall back on his butt. Then he'll do it again. Ten, twenty times. It's like watching an elephant learn to jump.

The caterpillars in Annie Dillard's *Pilgrim at Tinker Creek* march endlessly around the rim of a potted plant, each following chemical markers laid down by the one just ahead. Seven days. Straight. Pure will. That's Julian. Stand. Wobble. Fall. Stand. Wobble. Fall. His shock of blond hair doing its Andy Warhol thing. My caterpillar of a child.

VI

They have found a boy again in the weeds near Ohio, where the trains slow and clatter over the rails, the ties sounding out the rhythm of a dirge. I don't want to bring this in now, but the boy had his genitals cut off. Oh God, I don't want to say this. His trunk sliced to stripes of flesh, and the mottled glimpse of bone, his flesh turned the color of the swooping puzzle of the overpass. I don't want to make a bed of grief, to lie down in it again each night, but I have a son, and it is all I can do to hold him still beneath the ruined starlight.

VII

There are three of them playing in the sand. My son, a girl a year or so his elder and her brother pushing at the fences of two. The day is high and bright—fall careening down through the perfect density of blue. The girl's hair glissades as Julian tackles her. They laugh, splayed like fingers in the sand. The two-year-old doesn't understand the game and begins to scream. An intoxicating, wordless scream that goes on and on. Ten minutes pass and he will not be calmed, his face an umber work.

We finally separate them and move to go, pulling on our shoes and socks, the day falling beyond the shadow-sketching hills. The boy's mother brings him over to apologize, his *sorry* small and wet and barely healed. Julian leans in and with his tiny fist punches him, hard.

VIII

Now I am reading to my son with the remains of a rain still ticking off the fat catalpa leaves. My arms around him, the book before him on his knees.

Goodnight comb
And goodnight brush
Goodnight nobody
Goodnight mush.

Goodnight to the old lady
whispering hush.

Outside the window, beyond my son's quiet form, a road sign flashes in the blond grass, the vacant lot clumped with the rubble of old cars, a school bus up on blocks. Outside the window, the muted hills are torn with lines of the fall wheat-harvest, dust and fallow, the sky chalked with gray. Outside the window, the air is rich, the color of claret. Outside the window, my son . . . *hush*, I think . . . the weight of his life above him like moons, like stones.

Evolution

> *"the fledglings, the nest . . ."*
>
> —*Agamemnon*

It's a rabbit kit I find, her eyes
gone gauzy and fly-charmed
beneath the basil's redolent phalanx,
the thatch of thyme swarming
over the wall of Belgian block.
A rich scent rises from what
I've pushed aside, what crushed—
a Mediterranean ease as in light
caroming off verdigris water—
but all depth's gone from
her dead eyes, her walnut fur.
What killed her is another puzzle
I'll never turnstile through.
Still, it's hard not to wonder
what glossy machinery hums
inside this hand-sized carcass.
Whose sacrifice is being worked
out in this space splashed
by the scissor-blade shadows
of sumac and black walnut.

Warning

If I could find the beginning
of the story, get it down
from there, piece by piece,
assembled like the seawall
at Troy, the one Poseidon
feared. Or hated. It's hard
to tell. Blocks of stone
lashed by his wet hands.
His foaming beard
as he gnaws at the foundation.

There's a boy by the water's edge
slapping sand into wedges.
The sea grasses hiss when the wind
arrives hauling ships hived
with Myrmidons.
                      The boy
strips off his shirt and banners it
back and forth in the ripping wind.
Always the wind and the smell of cold.

Or Marie Antoinette waiting
naked in her sovereign bed
as her attendants pass a sentence
behind their hands. Maybe then
I could begin to explain. How it comes on.
Not without warning.

He Arranges His Poems

on the floor,
           the grid of a dig,
                      Pelmanism,
stonework,
        architecture of want.
                          Outside,
wind spindles
            among bare branches,
windows
        spiked with frost.
                      Black cherries
in a glass of syrah.
            Sweaty leather.
                      Pepper.
Books snigger
        from their shelves.
                      Early dark
trundles down around them.
                He could
sit there all night
            and nothing
                      would be made clear,
except the bruised globe
            of the wine.
And what good
            would it do
                      to rail
against the arched
            and cautious world,

    the world
            so stingy
                    with its gifts
    that weather
            becomes
                    a kind of miracle?
    The weather.
            Honestly,
                  he doesn't even know
                what to ask for anymore.
    The wind rises
            or dies
                  in the weltering cold.
    Leaves tick
            along the pavement
                      like clocks.
    Snow begins to fall.
            Or not.
                  It all depends
    on the arrangement.

Trust

When my son, now worn
and scrubbed and toweled dry
turns his head against the couch,
so close to sleep that sleep
seems suddenly easy, welcome
as skin, I lift him, his generous
body against mine and climb
the stairs to his room, the bed
prepared like a ship moored
among the wreckage of the day's
play—buckets and trucks
and the wild green eyes of Hope
the Dinosaur. I lift him from
my shoulder and hold him
in the air, balancing
his risky weight as he turns
toward the pillows he cannot see.

Desire

In the pre-dawn dark I rise to write
and wait for the first chirp of the alarm
that wakes my wife and drags her
from bed. The trees are just beginning
to distinguish themselves, the sky
the color of blue slate. I am working
on blue slate. I am working on the trees,
their branches slurred with fog.
I am working on honesty. On
the oriel-call that comes to my window.
The first burn of fall that crisps
the maples. I am working on the forms
that crawl so steadily out of the dark.
My own desire most of all. The faucet
squawks and water trundles in the tub.
The morning takes form around her,
steam and light and a smeared space
of clarity appearing in the mirror.

Not Resurrection

The pool's an envelope of blue
below the gracious hillside.
Georgian restraint and
the pungent air of summer
in St. Louis. Hydrangeas
elbow through the fence
and the clutch of honeysuckle
on the wind. Suddenly

I'm in too deep.
The aqua swale of water
above my eyes. The world ripples.
Jack's mother, her hair still
so Jackie O in '74, this fragile year,
dives out—arms arrowed,
hips tight as light.

It would be easy to say
that this is about renovation,
the diva churning out
the aria of a changed life.
The glitter of spit charged
with gold in the summer air
as I am lifted from the water
reborn. That's not
what I remember. Grace
and towering trees, her body
crossing the air between us,
that's what I recall. Not
the sinking, not the water

giving way. Not resurrection,
but the fine glimmer
of the water reflected
on her face as she crossed
the space between us.

York Harbor

> *A dragon lives forever,*
> *But not so little boys . . .*

If there are dragons in the world, they lie
down on the body of the river like fog.
Their bodies froth in the cold morning air,
the rising sun tearing at their wings
as boats clutch at each other in the harbor.
My son has dreamed badly and climbs into
my bed in the fragile cabin we share.
The light up early over the ocean. Stone
and water. *A dragon was eating my hair*,
he whimpers. I hush him, but everything
I would do to keep the wind from the door
is doomed. He turns back to sleep, stretching
his long legs into the warmth I've made.
I know this now: I will lose my son and
I will find him. No morning will equal
this morning and many will, many will.

An Elegy for the Living in Early Spring

When skunk cabbage unfurls
through the crusted snow
and ruffled cover, you know

it has come, suddenly,
like the appearance of robins.
Crocuses will open and moss green

the limestone along Bonne Homme Creek.
Across our field, its broken grass
still sheer from winter's blade,

a hawk hunts a lean snowshoe;
swoop and arc, stall and dive
following stutters through the fallow.

The hare's body pumps like a heart
when it pauses, keens pale
as a summer sky, pulled

from the earth and draped across
the black willow's still bare branches.
David tested positive and twenty years

flushed up in his face. For days he held on
to anger, stalked through rooms
of denial then abruptly he was gone,

caught a plane for Paris where he drank
cheap wine, pissed in the Seine
and bought beers for young blond boys

he wanted to kiss full on the mouth.
He left for Thailand, but before
arriving, walked through Leningrad

in a wind cold and hard and traded Levi's
that no longer fit for a Russian officer's hat
itself two sizes too small.

Near the floating market in Bangkok
he ate steamed rice and strips
of smoked pig. He smoked Pakistani hash

and passed his father's watch
to a man in dark cotton
who'd never owned one.

He arrived home telling stories,
gaunt and tan as autumn,
years older. We drank whiskey

against a San Francisco sunset,
talking of the pleasure we buy
with a little bit of death. I kissed

his mottled face and left for home
at dawn, Venus large and clean
on the western horizon.

Notes

Design

The two paintings referenced are Pieter Breughel the Elder's *The Massacre of the Innocents* and Domenico Ghirlandaio's *Slaughter of the Innocents*. Each depicts the mass killing of children ordered by Herod in his attempt to kill the Christ child.

Camera Obscura

Special forces loyal to former Yugoslav leader Slobodan Milosevic burned the bodies of hundreds of ethnic Albanians in a blast furnace before pulling out of Kosovo ahead of NATO troops. Men involved in the clandestine operation, which was intended to cover up atrocities that could lead to war crimes charges, said up to 1,500 bodies were burned at the Trepca lead refinery. Because they were too big to fit in the furnace, the bodies were first put in a grinder used for ore processing before being placed on the furnace conveyor belt. (AP) Celebici was a notorious prison camp where Bosnian Serbs were routinely raped, tortured, and killed in 1992. The text is from *The Oresteia*, by Aeschylus (*Complete Greek Tragedies*, 2nd ed., translated by Richmond Lattimore. University of Chicago Press, 1991; eds. Grene and Lattimore).

Bu Topraklar Bizimdir: A Message from Lefkosa

As far back as 280 BCE a walled city stood in the Mesaoria plain on the island of Cyprus; its name was Lefkosa. (The modern name of Nicosia arose in the 19th century.) Today that city stands on a U.N. buffer zone between the Turkish controlled area to the north and the southern Greek Cypriot half to the south. The text from the postcard—*Bu Topraklar Bizimdir*—can be roughly translated, *This Land is Ours*!

The Buddha

"When he recalled all his own births and deaths in all these previous lives of his, the Sage, full of pity, turned his compassionate mind towards other living beings, and he thought to himself: 'Again and again they must leave the people they regard as their own, and must go on elsewhere, and that without ever stopping. Surely this world is unprotected and helpless, and like a wheel it turns round and round.'" (From the *Buddhacarita* of Asvaghosha. Original translation from E. Conze, *Buddhist Texts through the Ages*. Oxford University Press, 1954).

Alcibiades Leaving North Avenue Beach

"For never did fortune surround and enclose a man with so many of those things which we vulgarly call goods, or so protect him from every weapon of philosophy, and fence him from every access of free and searching words, as she did Alcibiades; who, from the beginning, was exposed to the flatteries of those who sought merely his gratification, such as might well unnerve him, and indispose him to listen to any real adviser or instructor." —Plutarch.

Goodnight Nobody

The text is from *Goodnight Moon* by Margaret Wise Brown. Illustrations by Clement Hurd (New York: HarperCollins, 1947).

This poem is dedicated to my son, Julian, and Scott Drake, whose dismembered body was found in a grass and shrub-covered lot directly across from East Ohio Street in Pittsburgh.

Prayer

The text is from *The Oresteia*, by Aeschylus (*Complete Greek Tragedies*, 2nd ed., translated by Richmond Lattimore. University of Chicago Press, 1991; eds. Grene and Lattimore).

York Harbor

"Puff the Magic Dragon." Words and Music by Lenny Lipton and Peter Yarrow. © 1963; Renewed 1991 Honalee Melodies (ASCAP) and Silver Dawn Music (ASCAP).

Index of First Lines

Because it all begins with story   *3*
Bells of the Epiphany blend with sirens   *5*
Ends with angels roiling the air   *23*
Every poet knows   *18*
Fall's first gold has gone to rust   *43*
Japanese maples light up   *7*
I am reading this into precision   *22*
I have not written about my son's future   *31*
I, I start   *35*
If I could find the beginning   *56*
If there are dragons in the world, they lie   *63*
I run through this feud all day   *17*
In the coffeehouse   *11*
In the ninth month of my son's life   *29*
In the pre-dawn dark I rise to write   *60*
It has happened again   *45*
It is Hector who lingers near   *26*
It's always ashes and the blazing sun   *25*
It's a rabbit kit I find, her eyes   *55*
My father sanding ash   *39*
My wife's new shoes hiss like cats   *14*
On the postcard, crescent and star   *9*
on the floor   *57*
She has unwrapped the gates of hell   *28*
Sunlight reflected   *37*
Surely this world is unprotected and helpless   *27*
The el track's staccato shadows   *33*
The lake burnished   *41*
The late afternoon light settles down around them   *47*
The plane descending   *20*

The pool's an envelope of blue   *61*
The sound of my son asleep   *34*
This the point where it begins—   *16*
When a late rain has turned   *46*
When my son, now worn   *59*
When skunk cabbage unfurls   *64*
When you have been a long time gone   *44*

About the Author

Jeffrey Thomson's first collection of poetry, *The Halo Brace*, was published by Birch Brook Press and *Renovation*, his third book, is forthcoming from Carnegie Mellon University Press. He has also published poetry and nonfiction in *Quarterly West, New Delta Review, Puerto del Sol, Gulf Coast,* and *Willow Springs*, as well as critical essays on Sandra Cisneros, James Wright, Derek Walcott and the environmental elegy. He has been a Fellow at the Writers @ Work Conference and a Tennessee Williams Scholar at the Sewanee Writers Conference. His works have won numerous awards, including the Master's Poetry Contest and the Academy of American Poets' Prize on three occasions. He received his PhD from the University of Missouri in Creative Writing in 1996 and is currently an Assistant Professor of English at Chatham College in Pittsburgh where he directs the MFA in Writing program.